A Boy & His Baseball

THE DAVE DRAVECKY STORY

by Judy Gire

illustrated by Joan Holub

ZondervanPublishingHouse
Grand Rapids, Michigan

A Division of HarperCollinsPublishers

A Boy and His Baseball
Text copyright © 1992 by Judy Gire
Illustrations copyright © 1992 by Joan Holub

Zondervan Publishing House
Grand Rapids, Michigan 49530

Library of Congress Cataloging-in-Publication Data

Gire, Judy.
   A boy and his baseball : the Dave Dravecky story / by Judy Gire.
     p. cm.
   Summary: Describes the role of faith and hard work in the fulfillment
of Dave Dravecky's dream to become a major league pitcher and in his
fight against cancer.
   ISBN 0-310-58630-5
   1. Dravecky, Dave—Juvenile literature. 2. Baseball players—United
States—Biography—Juvenile literature. [1. Dravecky, Dave. 2. Baseball
players. 3. Cancer—Patients. 4. Christian life.] I. Title.
GV865.D66G57 1992
796.357′092—dc20
[B]   92-15580
                                           CIP
                                           AC

Published in association with Sealy M. Yates, Orange, California

Cover design by Jack Foster
Interior design by Christine Hoffman
Edited by David Lambert

Printed in the United States of America

01 02 03 04 05 06 / BP / 10 9 8 7 6 5 4 3 2

This edition is printed on acid-free paper
and meets the American National Standards Institute Z39.48 standard.

To Ken,
Of all the wonderful thoughts
I have of us,
thoughts of the years ahead
warm me the most.
—J.G.

For George,
with love and thanks.
—J.H.

Every winter in Youngstown, Ohio, snow shuts down the Little League ball fields. For young Dave Dravecky, it was a prison sentence—three months without baseball.

As Dave sat in class, his thoughts wandered. They traveled over the spluttering radiator ... through the window laced with frost ... and on toward the ball field.

There he saw a bundled-up bunch of children playing. One flopped onto the pitcher's mound. With her arms and legs, she etched an angel in the snow. Others threw snowballs at the backstop. One boy's stray pitch smacked a little girl in the face and sent her crying to her mother.

Dave smiled and thought, *Yes, sports fans, it looks like a long day for the home team as the pitcher walks another batter!*

But his laughter soon turned into longing for spring. He imagined a field of freshly mowed grass. And he imagined himself walking onto that field. When he did, it changed, as if by magic, into a big-league ballpark—a ballpark where the big boys played.

The crowd cheered him all the way to the pitcher's mound. As he stepped onto the mound, the crowd hushed.

Dave rolled the ball in his fingers, feeling the raised seams. He lifted his glove to his face. That glove had been a long-time friend, and the smell of its leather warmed him. He hurled the ball past the batter. Swing and a miss! The crowd roared and—"Clank, clank, hissssssss." The radiator scolded him, yanking his thoughts back to the classroom.

Spring finally came to Youngstown. And Dave was there with glove in hand to greet it.

Spring after spring, he pitched.

And winter after winter, he dreamed of someday playing in the big leagues.

As a Little Leaguer, Dave concentrated on striking out one batter at a time. When he was eleven, he pitched his first no-hitter against one of the toughest teams in town.

When he was sixteen, he played on a hometown team three days a week. But he wanted to play *every* day. So he joined another team in nearby Pennsylvania. That way, he could play three days in Ohio and three days in Pennsylvania.

During Dave's last year in college, two things brought him closer to that dream. First, he married his high-school

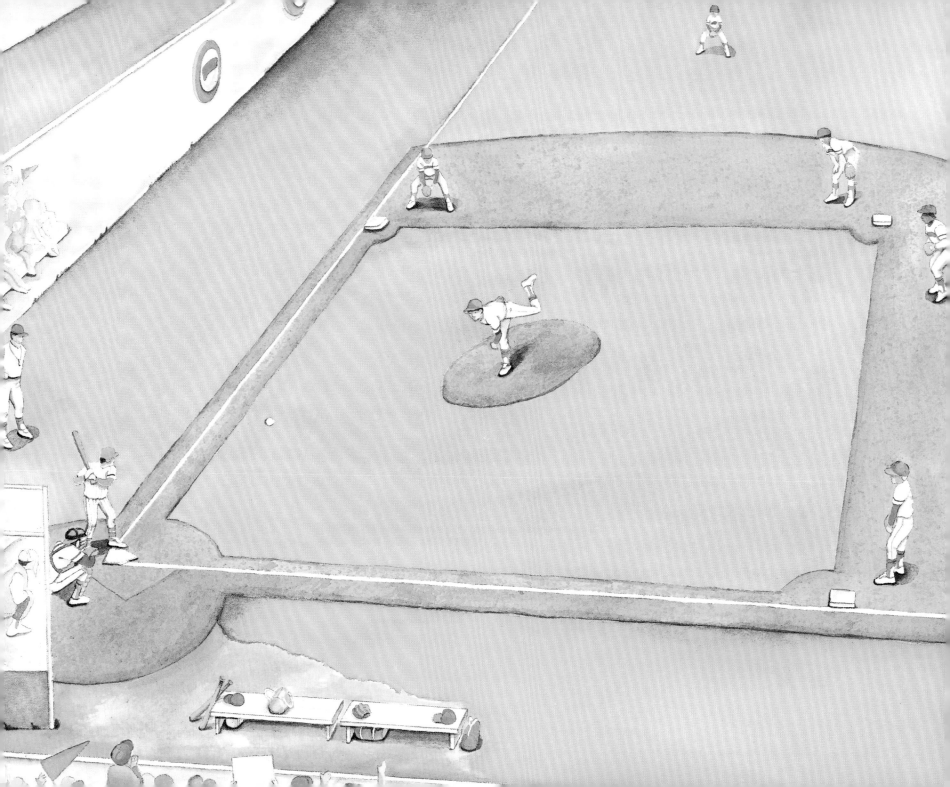

sweetheart, Janice. Second, he was asked to play ball for a minor-league team.

He worked hard in the minor leagues, strengthening his arm and learning to control the ball. After three years in the minors, he was named Player of the Year.

Then came a call from the San Diego Padres: "We need you, Dave. You're coming to the big leagues!"

Dave's dream was finally coming true. He was so eager that he asked the cab driver to take him straight from the airport to the Padres' clubhouse.

In the cab, Dave wondered how his new teammates would welcome him. After all, he had been dreaming of this moment all his life! Maybe there would even be a band to announce his arrival!

There was no band. When he entered the clubhouse, only a few players bothered to greet him.

Dave began to worry. *Why did I even come here?* he wondered. *Do I really belong here?*

When the Padres saw Dave pitch, they weren't sure he belonged there either.

Dave came to the big leagues expecting to feel like a professional baseball player. Instead, he felt like a little boy—a little boy who was expected to do a man's job. He was afraid. He wasn't throwing strikes like he used to. And he

couldn't figure out why.

Dave's lowest point came when he pitched in TV's Game of the Week at Candle-stick Park. TV cameras were everywhere. *Oh great,* he thought. *Now everyone in the world can watch me flub up.*

When Dave was called in to pitch, runners were already on base. He walked slowly to the mound. He tried to concentrate, but the noise of the crowd distracted him. He threw the first pitch.

"Ball one!" the umpire shouted.

Dave looked to his catcher for a signal, but he couldn't understand it. He threw

the second pitch.

"Ball two!"

Sweat trickled down his face. He threw again.

"Ball three!"

His eyes stung with humiliation as he took off his cap and wiped the sweat away. The crowd booed. He took a deep breath, trying to ignore them. He fired a fourth pitch to the batter.

"Ball four!"

Walking the batter was *the worst* thing he could have done. The crowd chanted, "Throw strikes, you bum!"

He was trying to throw strikes, but he was failing. He knew it. The crowd knew it. And thanks to the television cameras, *everyone* knew it.

When he trudged through the door of his home, Janice could see that he was upset. "What's wrong?" she asked.

"My dream has turned into a nightmare," Dave said. "I can't throw strikes anymore. And if I can't throw strikes, my days in the big leagues are over."

"Why can't you throw strikes?" she asked.

"When I get on the mound, I lose control of my arm. I start thinking, *I'm in the big leagues now. These are big-league batters.* And I can't concentrate. I hear everything the crowd is saying. I get the heebie jeebies." He paused and looked into her eyes. "I'm scared, Janice."

She put her arms around him. "What are you afraid of?"

Dave shrugged. "I'm letting the fans down, for one thing. And my teammates. And our manager."

"Dave," Janice said, "you'll never be able to do enough to please them. There's only one person you need to please, and that's Jesus Christ. Pitch as though he were the only one watching you. He'll be pleased—even if you don't throw strikes."

The next time Dave pitched, he took Janice's advice. For the first time since he had come to the big leagues, baseball became fun again! And even better, he started throwing strikes.

Dave never forgot Janice's words. It was advice he would need in the months ahead—when again he would lose control of his arm.

Dave's pitching soon caught the attention of the San Francisco Giants. That team made a deal with the Padres, and in 1987, Dave moved to San Francisco and put on a Giants uniform.

Shortly after he began playing for the Giants, Dave noticed a small lump on

his pitching arm. At first, he wasn't concerned. But the lump grew larger, so large that even his teammates noticed it: "Man, that lump is getting bigger than your arm!"

The Giants' doctor checked the lump. He was worried; he wanted Dave to see a specialist.

Dave and Janice went to a clinic where pictures were taken of the inside of his arm. As they sat in the waiting room, they could hear the doctors' voices: "Look at the size of that tumor!"

Dave and Janice looked at each other. "I think we need to pray," Janice said.

They held hands as Dave prayed: "Dear God, we don't know what's happening, but whatever it is, help us to get through it."

The doctor came into the room. "I want to take a sample of that lump," he said. "We have to find out if it is cancerous."

Dave and Janice were stunned. *Cancerous?*

The sample from the tumor was sent to a lab. After a week, Dave and Janice went back to the clinic.

"As we suspected," the doctor said calmly. "This tumor is cancerous." He took out a piece of paper and drew a picture. It showed how the tumor, attached to the bone of Dave's upper left arm, had also spread into the muscles.

"When we operate," the doctor said, "we'll have to take out more than just the tumor. We'll have to cut out all the muscle surrounding it."

"How long will it be before I can pitch again, Doc?"

"Dave, you'll be losing the use of the most powerful muscle in your arm," said the doctor.

"What about my career?"

"After this operation," the doctor said, "even simple things will be hard for you to do. You probably won't even be able to reach into your back pocket and take out your wallet."

"In other words," Janice said, "short of a miracle, he will never pitch again."

"That's right," said the doctor. "Short of a miracle, he will never pitch again."

For the rest of the 1988 season, Dave stayed at home, recovering from surgery. The closest he came to a baseball game was watching it on TV—as he did the night of the final game of the World Series.

The TV screen sent flickerings of light against the darkened room where Dave sat on a couch. He tried to get comfortable, cradling an arm that throbbed with pain. Janice was in bed, asleep, and Dave felt lonely.

When the last inning ended, the winning team raced to the mound and threw their arms around their pitcher. The only thing that raced to Dave was a crowd of depressing thoughts: *The season started out so well. It could have been me out there on that mound. It could have been me.*

Sitting slumped on the couch, staring at the television, Dave realized that his boyhood dream was over. His arm ached, but the ache in his heart hurt far worse. And for the first time since the tumor had been discovered, he cried.

A few weeks later, Dave began physical therapy. At first, his arm moved slowly. Then, to his surprise, simple movements started coming back.

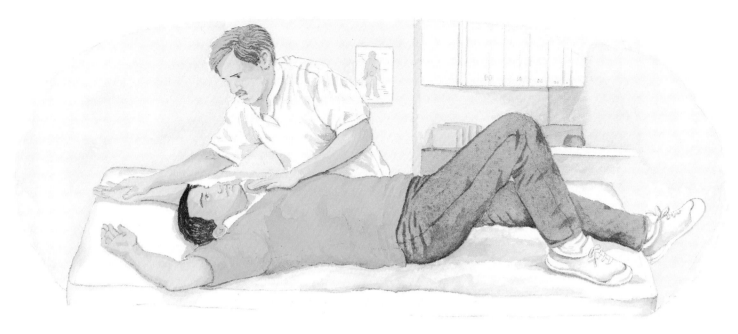

Week after week he continued the strenuous exercises.

And week after week his arm got stronger.

After five weeks of therapy, Dave came home grinning. "Watch this," he told Janice, and with his left hand he reached slowly into his back pocket and pulled out his wallet.

Janice got so excited she began to cry.

"That's not all," he said. He stood for a moment, as if he were on a pitcher's mound. Then, holding an imaginary ball, he went through the motion of pitching.

Janice stared, her eyes swollen with tears. "I can't believe it."

When Dave returned to the clinic in New York for his three-month checkup, he couldn't wait to show the doctor his progress.

"Okay, Dave, show me what you can do," the doctor said.

Dave stretched his arm over his head.

"Wow," said the doctor.

Then Dave put his hands at his side and pushed both arms straight back.

The doctor's eyes opened wide in amazement.

"Well, Doc, what do you think? Will I be able to pitch again?"

The doctor grew serious. "It's risky for you to even try to pitch now. Your arm needs more time to heal."

"Could I just toss the ball around a little at spring training?" The doctor was hesitant. "Come on, Doc," Dave pleaded.

Finally, the doctor agreed. Dave flew back in time for the last week of spring training. His teammates flocked around him to take a look at his arm. When Dave moved his arm through the pitching motions, they cheered.

Dravecky was back!

But the Giants' trainer wasn't so sure. He could see how far Dave had to go before he'd be ready for a comeback.

"Dave, you need to think like a prize fighter training for the biggest fight of his life," he said. "The prize is a chance to pitch again."

But after three months of grueling therapy, the trainer was amazed at Dave's progress.

"It's a miracle. I don't understand how it happened, but you're ready to pitch again."

Dave tested his arm by pitching in some minor-league games. He looked good. So good that the Giants scheduled his comeback game for August 10, 1989, against the Cincinnati Reds.

On that day, the walls at Candlestick Park were lined with photographers. As Dave walked onto the field, hundreds of cameras flashed in his face.

What's going on? he wondered.

Suddenly the ballpark exploded with noise. As Dave's eyes adjusted to the light, he squinted into the stands. The fans were on their feet—thirty-four thousand of them—on their feet and yelling like crazy.

When he got to the bullpen and started warming up, the crowd noise died down. But when he walked to the dugout, the fans jumped to their feet a second time, cheering and shouting their encouragement:

"Go get 'em, Dave!"

"We're glad you're back!"

And when he walked to the mound to begin the game, they stood and cheered again! He looked at the stadium full of people. He could see Janice among them, standing and cheering. He waved his cap in gratitude. He looked over his shoulder; the scoreboard beamed in huge letters:

WELCOME BACK, DAVE!

He stepped off the mound and bowed his head to thank God for the opportunity to play once again the game he loved so much.

When Dave stepped back onto the mound, a hush fell over the crowd. He rolled the ball in his hand, feeling its raised seams—those same, familiar seams he had felt since he was a little boy. He lifted the glove to his face, smelling its leather—that same, familiar smell he had grown up with, spring after spring in Ohio.

He hurled the ball past the batter. And past the next batter. And the next.

Three up, three down. When he ran to the dugout, the crowd again rose to their feet and cheered.

Each time Dave came to the mound, he threw strikes. And each time he left that mound, the fans stood and cheered.

In the eighth inning, the Reds gained three runs against the Giants' four. Dave knew that the manager would send in a relief pitcher for the ninth inning. The crowd sensed that Dave was finished for the day. They stood again and cheered wildly as he walked to the dugout.

The relief pitcher went to the mound to begin the ninth inning. He would pitch

well, and the Giants would win the game, four to three. But before he delivered his first pitch, the crowd started clapping and calling for Dave.

Dave couldn't remember being so happy as he walked onto the field. Looking into the stands, he could see row after row of yelling fans. Hats and handkerchiefs were waving wildly. Cheers followed cheers as he walked back to the dugout.

But the fans would not stop. They wanted him to come out onto the field again. In the dugout, Dave's teammates motioned him to go back out.

"Go on out there," they said. "It's your day. Take a bow."

Again he stepped onto the field and raised his cap to the crowd.

It *was* his day.

A day beyond his wildest boyhood dreams.

And on that day, above the roar of the crowd, he could hear the applause of heaven.

Many are the dreams in a young man's heart,

but it is the plan of God that will be established.

(paraphrase of Proverbs 19:21)

After Dave's dramatic comeback game, God's plan for Dave's life proceeded in a different way than Dave had ever dreamed.

Five days after his comeback victory against the Cincinnati Reds, Dave was pitching against the Montreal Expos when his left arm broke. It broke a second time when he was caught in a crush of teammates celebrating the win that sent the Giants to the World Series.

He never pitched again.

Dave retired from baseball at the end of the 1989 season. After his retirement, he underwent three more surgeries. The first one was to remove another tumor in his pitching arm and most of the remaining muscle. The second was to graft muscle from his back onto his arm. And sadly,

the third surgery was to amputate the arm after repeated attempts had failed to stop infection and pain.

Through all these surgeries, his fans continued to cheer and pray for him.

They continue still.

Dave Dravecky's boyhood dream of playing in the big leagues came true in a most remarkable way.

But that dream is over.

Now he dreams a new dream—that all who hear his story will live their lives as though Jesus Christ were the only one watching. Because *his* applause is all that really matters.